They Still Call Us Witches

poems by

Anne Gottlieb

Finishing Line Press
Georgetown, Kentucky

They Still Call Us Witches

Copyright © 2025 by Anne Gottlieb
ISBN 979-8-89990-259-8 First Edition
All rights reserved under International and Pan-American Copyright Conventions. No part of this book may be reproduced in any manner whatsoever without written permission from the publisher, except in the case of brief quotations embodied in critical articles and reviews.

ACKNOWLEDGMENTS

This work could not have been born without the incomparable Terrance Hayes creating the golden shovel form and the iconic poetry of Gwendolyn Brooks. The work could not have been completed without the love and support of Eli, Dean, Asher, Mom, Dad, Paul, David, and Peter. Thank you to my friends and first readers, some that love poetry and some that hate it but read it anyway.

Publisher: Leah Huete de Maines
Editor: Christen Kincaid
Cover Art: Dean Gottlieb
Author Photo: Dean Gottlieb
Cover Design: Elizabeth Maines McCleavy

Order online: www.finishinglinepress.com
also available on amazon.com

Author inquiries and mail orders:
Finishing Line Press
PO Box 1626
Georgetown, Kentucky 40324
USA

Contents

They still call us witches, among other things 1

What You Are 2

The Lessons 3

Reflection 4

Fragile 5

The Switch 6

Fold Over Woman 7

A Mother's Dream 8

School Board Candidate Forum 9

Renewal 10

Motherhood 11

Knowing 12

Disunion 13

Leaving 14

Honey 15

Rock Bottom 16

The Wheels 17

The Longing 18

The Circle 19

> "one day we can dance in the forest
> and in the streets
> and with each other
> in our rooms that belong to us and only to us
> on our beds we share with no one
> under the moon
> under the sun
> under the shade of our favorite trees"

—Kimberly Belflower, "John Proctor is the Villain"

All the following poems are golden shovels. This form was created by Terrance Hayes using a line from the Gwendolyn Brooks poem, "We Real Cool." Each word from the line from the original poem serves as the last word in each line of the new poem. If the reader reads the last word in each line, she will be reading the line from the original poem.

All original poems and authors are listed under the title of my new poem.

They still call us witches, among other things

After "A Woman Speaks" by Audre Lorde

Our bodies have always been tethered to the moon.
Pale radiance pulling and pushing our insides. Marked

with blood by Mother Nature's own precious palms and
condemned to Man's misunderstanding. Born touched

and dipped in Her incandescence. Man drawn in by
our orbit until He seeks to eclipse our brilliance. The

eventide glow will always persist and always rival the sun.

What You Are

After "Wolfpack" by Abby Wambach

For so long you
never knew what you were.
You threw like a girl but never
wore the pink dresses and little
ribbons. Your knees skinned red
in the summer from clumsily riding
your skateboard with your hood
up over your head, hiding. You
felt like the kind of girl you were
wasn't allowed in the club. Always
looking in on the tea party from the
window until you realized you were the wolf.

The Lessons

After "weaponed woman" by Gwendolyn Brooks

At recess, the boys scurry outside to the basketball courts but
she is told she can't go and learns her first lesson of the 6th grade. She
watches from the doorway as they flail and holler. A tear fights
its way out stinging her flushed face filled with confusion and
contempt. *Has everyone always known these rules but me?* Has
she ever been ashamed to be who she is? On that day she fought
no one, but sat inside at the lunch table with all of the girls, according
to the way things had always been done. She went to
the try-outs for the girls team but still sharpened her
skills with neighbor boys into the night with the car lights
flooding the driveway. When they stripped the ball and
blocked her shots, she knew she was learning the
ways to be a better player. She didn't want lenience
when they played, she wanted to beat all of
them. In time, she blocked shots and stole the ball back. Sometimes, her
destiny was hers. This was the second lesson. The whirling-
world around her would never again so easily put her in her place.

Reflection

After "I'm Just A Girl" by Gwen Stefani and Thomas Dumont

I stop to check myself in the mirror. My appearance is about what
they want. The push-up bra and heavy, red lips, I've
learned, catch their attention. My friends and I succumbed
so long ago, I can't even remember trying to
be something else. But I know she is

still in me. The ten-year-old girl playing ball with her brothers, making
one shot after another in the driveway. I was me

before I was numb.

Fragile

After "Killing Methods" by Ada Limon

He drapes his arm over my shoulder so
his fingers brush against my breast. I
am a stranger to this hand. And ready to kill
the appendage and its owner but I only push it
away. *You're not that pretty anyway.* His words pin
my teenage self-esteem to the shadows with its
husky growl, masking his wound from my terrible
bite. I think twice the next time. I hide my wings.
I taste the bile in my mouth and then swallow it down.

The Switch

After "Citizen: An American Lyric" by Claudia Rankine

"Sweetheart," drips thickly from his lips, as if we
are lovers, the word tugging me to come back to bed. My ears suffer

and my synapses react to the intimate ownership from
a stranger. Inwardly, I recoil away from the

poison. But outwardly I have been educated, condition(ed)
to ingratiate myself, automatically flipping the word to a term of

endearment that I pretend to enjoy as flattery. Meanwhile, my true being
chokes in the back of my throat so that I can remain acceptable,
    addressable.

Fold Over Woman

From "Beskikwe" (Fold-Over Woman) by Lois Beardslee

With the vow also comes the fold-over,
expectations of Wife turns Woman
into half. Less than when she cries.
Fullness regained only when he is out
She sits at the piano, banging the notes loud.
Has forgotten why she stopped playing and
now pressing all the way into the keys while sound thunders
through her breastbone all the way to the back
of her skull. Rattling and shaking, he finds her at
the piano and hesitantly touches her shoulder. Her head turns, eyes
    clouded.
She stills, stands, smooths her apron and folds over,
with less flexibility under unexceptional skies.

A Mother's Dream

> *After "An Atlas of the Difficult World XIII (Dedications)"*
> *by Adrienne Rich*

You stir thick gravy, warming.
Farmhands wash the fields off their fingers. Glasses of fresh milk
already set on the table. Everyday a
dinner party for twenty. You hold a crying

toddler in your arms, another at your skirt, and another child
in a crib wide awake. Neediness and chicken pox linger on
all of you. You do not immediately recognize when your
days are not your own. You scrub the grout until your shoulder

grows numb in hopes that your mother will not see a
failure. Where is the book,
you wonder, to explain how you arrived in
this surreal place that is your
home, your loved ones, your hand.

School Board Candidate Forum

*After NYT headline by Alexis Soloski, print edition,
March 28, 2021*

Necklace, clutch, gloss, phone. She,
walks into the event, the only female candidate in a field of six, and is
unseen. Doctorate, school principal, experienced, versatile.
Smiles, nods and shakes hands, but is not
asked any questions of consequence. Instead, *how will you have the
    time?* an
endless drone, asked of no man. Decoration, token, bauble, accessory.

Renewal

After "Willing in the Orisha" by Camonghne Felix

In the stillness of pre-dawn twilight my
mind hums, loosening limbs through my body,
following a fatter frequency than light laden day. A
calling at this hour comes at full
volume that only I hear. Bass strings echo
my insides. Thrumming and warming. I
sway, my legs moving on their own. I dawdle
out to the darkness and dew, meandering down
the soft, crushed grass with bare feet to
hear myself better. My body takes me to the
soothing flow of water over rocks at the moonlit creek.

Motherhood

After "Lessons" by Grace Fondow

Three little bodies settle into seats as I look outside the kitchen
 window. I see a
day before daybreak and I vow never to eat oatmeal in the dark again.
 The loop

of stay-at-home time with toddlers has unfurled as an upside-down
 yellow brick road. Our
journey won't end with a wizard. I am the only one here, trying to
 savor these experiences

as my mother commands me. But she comes and goes as she pleases.
 My days coincide
closer to the Tin Man, so many beating hearts but I can't feel my own.
 Searching to collide

with something beyond the days we are all in tears. I try to accept the
 solitude. I swallow
shame and goldfish in the same gulp. Putting one foot in front of
 another to keep on this

path that I wished for, knowing they are growing fast, not knowing I
 would want otherness.

Knowing

After "emergency warning" by Yrsa Daley-Ward

Squirreling away moments of time like little
secrets. Solitude becoming acts of rebellions.
Hiding behind headaches that are causing
canyons lined with raging rivers of chaos.
Letting vows float away and finally sink in-
to the undertow until I am what is left. I am all.

Disunion

> *After "the world is about to end, and my grandparents are in love" by Kara Jackson*

"Who will take me to school?" wondered the
youngest son at the epicenter of the subject.

"I will, like I take you now." Motherhood spoke and salvaged,
as She will do when there is no other way out. She comforts by

scooping up and bundling together the
remnants of things. I know that Her tent

cannot fix the earthquake I have made of
my life. But I let Motherhood distract their

disorientation until laughter vibrates across our tongues.

Leaving

After "Marriage as Death" by Kate Baer

Waiting for the judge, I remember my parents walking me down
the freshly mowed path in the sweltering afternoon heat. The
chilly, narrow courtroom holds tables and chairs that create sterile aisles,
dissolution not adorned with borrowed earrings or bouquets of flowers.
My lawyers keep me steady today when the magistrate calls on
me. Then forever is cut down with the quick scrawl of them
pens. Nothing left to say or see so we put on our coats.

Honey
    After "What You Pray Toward" by Patricia Smith

When the social construction of Love ended for me, I
furiously rejected it back. Fuck you, Love. What the fuck was
that? But I have never been able to stay angry and sneaking
in was the feeling that Love had done me a favor. Love ending gave
    me time.
To explore my broken pieces where I laid. To examine the legs with
which I stood up. The same Love cannot grow again, I know. My
love dreams in new colors and pulses from deep inside. I have made
    it my own
first. Love glows when I give it away and when I spread it all over my
    body.

Rock Bottom

After "Tiny Garden" by Jamila Woods

When I face the bathroom mirror, it's
still my skin, chickenpox scars and all, not
a crease out of place. Where are the butterflies
I promised myself. No washbasin baptism or
time ticking forward has ever meant fireworks
and home free. *Use your lungs*, my voice said.
Pushing all the air out, she spoke again, it's
cultivating, not lightning. You're gonna
sit with the shadows and stillness. You will be
stony seeds in the cool mud. Until a
dawn comes to warm you. Until a tiny
sprout pushes through. Until you become a garden.

The Wheels
After "Her Kind" by Anne Sexton

I tell myself it was just a touch and
some words and try to swallow my
confusion. Remind myself that my ribs
are only my own. But each offense is a crack
against my courage. There is nowhere
to hide where I will not find your
predatory kind. The wonted wheels
continue to wound and wind.

Again, your assault is excused and
the judge, the reporters, my
brother and father remind me my ribs
have never been my own. They crack
but do not break. Heal stronger where
the fissures are found. Until your
tropes whine like rusty wheels.
your promises scatter like dead leaves in the wind.

You sit in a glass carriage and
perpetuate your bidding to bend my
convictions, crushing my ribs.
I lie in wait to find a crack
in the familiar parade where
my destiny will disrupt your
decree. My resolve will wedge the wheels
and send you sailing into the wind.

The Longing

*After "When You Have Forgotten Sunday: the love story"
by Gwendolyn Brooks*

Soft breath of my name at dawn and
A tug at my arm, showing me how
To keep the rising sun from turning time, we
Lost limbo lazy lush, lay finally
Embracing an otherwise elusive state of undressed-
Ness. Over rumpled pillows and
Under towering sheets like whipped
Butter. Barricaded bodies force day out
Lost limbo lazy lush, longingly the
Shards of half light
Lurk, moving the hours and
Long fingers flowed
Between open mouths, over heated skin, into
clenched hands. We pushed the world away in bed.

The Circle

After "amazons" by Lucille Clifton

When night falls. When
the cast comes. And they always do. The
jagged edged feathers and sharp beaks root out the rookery.
Stealth ambush seeks to scatter us to the edges of
antiquity. These predators do not know that women,
endowed with the armor of warriors
under every inch of skin, bonded with the blood of all
daughters that came before, each
offering their alms of endurance, cupping
the womb, the wounded, even the one
who does not feel worthy, have not one hand
but a nest of tendons and muscles around
us. To show the one that feels alone that her
strength will never succumb, our life force, always remaining,
beats in her breast.

Anne Gottlieb earned her EdD from National Louis University. She's been an educator in the Chicago area since 1995, including principal of Austin Career Education Center for nine years. During her time there, she enjoyed coaching students to participate in Louder Than A Bomb and taking students camping the most. She has been published in *Salon, East on Central* and *California English*, and writes a blog about being an empty nester with over one hundred loyal readers. She teaches high school English in Hillside, Illinois. The daughter of a professor and a librarian, she belongs to two book clubs and one writing group. In her free time, she enjoys watching her three sons play ultimate frisbee.

www.ingramcontent.com/pod-product-compliance
Lightning Source LLC
Chambersburg PA
CBHW022108080426
42734CB00009B/1512